stuff, be gone

Simple Steps to Organize and Manage Your Home

Zohra Mubeena

© **Copyright 2023 - All rights reserved.**

The content contained within this book may not be reproduced, duplicated or transmitted without direct written permission from the author or the publisher.

Under no circumstances will any blame or legal responsibility be held against the publisher, or author, for any damages, reparation, or monetary loss due to the information contained within this book, either directly or indirectly.

Legal Notice:

This book is copyright protected. It is only for personal use. You cannot amend, distribute, sell, use, quote or paraphrase any part, or the content within this book, without the consent of the author or publisher.

Disclaimer Notice:

Please note the information contained within this document is for educational and entertainment purposes only. All effort has been executed to present accurate, up to date, reliable, complete information. No warranties of any kind are declared or implied. Readers acknowledge that the author is not engaged in the rendering of legal, financial, medical or professional advice. The content within this book has been derived from various sources. Please consult a licensed professional before attempting any techniques outlined in this book.

By reading this document, the reader agrees that under no circumstances is the author responsible for any losses, direct or indirect, that are incurred as a result of the use of the information contained within this document, including, but not limited to, errors, omissions, or inaccuracies.

Table of Contents

INTRODUCTION 3
    THE IMPACT OF CLUTTER ON YOUR LIFE 4
    DISCOVER JOY IN A CLUTTER-FREE SPACE 7
    A LITTLE ABOUT MY JOURNEY 8
    HOW THIS BOOK WILL HELP 9

CHAPTER 1: YOUR DECLUTTERING JOURNEY 11
    MAKE SPACE FOR WHAT YOU NEED 11
    ASSESS YOUR CLUTTER 16
    CREATE A PLAN OF ACTION 18
    GATHER SUPPLIES 19
    SORT YOUR BELONGINGS 20
    DECIDE WHAT TO KEEP, DONATE, OR DISCARD 23
        Keep 24
        Donate 25
        Discard 26
    ASSESS SENTIMENTAL ITEMS 27

CHAPTER 2: ORGANIZING 29
    CREATE A DESIGNATED PLACE FOR EVERYTHING 29
        Kitchen and Pantry Organization 30
        Bedroom and Closet Organization 32
        Bathroom and Laundry Room Organization 34
        Living Room Organization 36
        Home Office and Study Space Organization 38
        Sentimental Collections 39
        Personal Photo Collections 40
    USE STORAGE SOLUTIONS AND ORGANIZATION SYSTEMS 42
        How to Choose an Organizational System 43
    MAXIMIZE SPACE AND EFFICIENCY 43

CHAPTER 3: CLEANING AND MAINTENANCE 45
    ESTABLISH A CLEANING ROUTINE 45
        Daily Cleaning 46
        Weekly Cleaning 47
        Monthly Cleaning 48
        Seasonal Cleaning 48

PREVENT CLUTTER FROM BUILDING UP 49
    One In, One Out *49*
    Paper Pile *50*
    All Hands on Deck *50*
TIPS FOR KEEPING YOUR HOME TIDY AND ORGANIZED 51

CHAPTER 4: MINDSET AND LIFESTYLE 53

THE CONNECTION BETWEEN CLUTTER AND MENTAL HEALTH 53
CREATING A CLUTTER-FREE LIFESTYLE 54
TIPS TO STAY ORGANIZED AND MINIMIZE FUTURE CLUTTER 56

CHAPTER 5: A QUICK REVIEW OF POPULAR DECLUTTERING METHODS 59

THE 5S METHOD 60
THE ONE-MINUTE RULE 61
THE FOUR-BOX METHOD 62
    The Trash Box *62*
    The Give Away Box *63*
    The Storage Box *63*
    The Put Away Box *63*
THE SIX-MONTH POLICY 64
THE KONMARI METHOD 65
THE DANSHARI METHOD 67
    Refuse *67*
    Dispose *67*
    Separate *68*
THE FUROSHIKI METHOD 68
THE SWEDISH DEATH CLEANING 71

THE JOURNEY FORWARD 73

ACKNOWLEDGMENTS 77

REFERENCES 79

IMAGE REFERENCES 83

In loving memory of my papa...without you, there is no me!

To my ma...without you, I cease to exist.

Introduction

The first step in crafting the life you want is to get rid of everything you don't.
—Joshua Becker

In this fast-paced, increasingly chaotic world, finding solace in a clutter-free space has become a vital pursuit. Society makes it seem like you must buy, buy, buy to keep up appearances. You should have the latest smartphone to send updated emojis to your friends and stay in touch with less effort! You need a new, safe car to lovingly transport your family from point A to point B! You could cook delicious dinners if only you had these handy kitchen gadgets!

We're bombarded with advertisements and social media posts touting so many materialistic items as the latest and greatest that we feel less than if we don't own them. However, many people find that once they buy these things, they don't magically feel better. Rather, they're just stuck with more stuff they won't use. I know people who can't resist buying a device that will make cooking easier than ever, only to use it twice and go back to their old ways. Some have cupboards full of kitchen devices that were supposed to change their lives, but all they did was crowd the kitchen counters until they were tucked out of sight. When I help these people clean their homes, I ask them to be honest about how often they've used the device and if it really helped their cooking. They never use the item enough to make it worth keeping, so we donate or sell it, and they learn not to fall for those wily advertisements again.

When it comes to my own stuff, I think back to the many clothes I was given that occupied space and added to my belongings. Some came as wedding gifts, some I bought, and others were heirlooms. I wanted to keep them for sentimental reasons, and because I never knew when I might need a certain garment. However, I decided to purge everything about five years ago. Now, my closet is better organized, and the shelves remain empty. I don't want to fill those up just because I have the space—I like knowing there is extra space in my home.

When I read *Atomic Habits* by James Clear, a concept stuck with me. The book talks about "resetting the room," or priming the environment for your future uses. Instead of cleaning up after yourself, you're preparing for what will come next. This simple thought was liberating. I didn't need permission to give away stuff—I needed to reset my space the way I wanted to live in it. I extended this philosophy to both my physical and mental space, giving birth to my mantra, "Habits in motion are habits in action."

Each time I thought of my mantra, I would reflect on my life experience with collecting and decluttering. After realizing that I had an extensive history in this field, I decided to write it all down to help others find the same peace that I've found in living a minimalist life.

This book is your compass, guiding you toward a more organized and harmonious home. I'll walk you through the entire organizing process using practical strategies, expert advice, and real-life insights from my own experiences. Following the guidelines in this book serves to clean your physical space and rejuvenate your mind and soul. With a clean, organized space around you, you'll finally feel the freedom of letting go of materialistic constraints. Before we jump into the practical application of decluttering, let's first take time to understand the impact *stuff* has on your life and how an organized space can set you free. I'll also share my history of decluttering so you'll have an idea of how my experiences have colored my approach to this minimalist lifestyle I so enjoy.

The Impact of Clutter on Your Life

Clutter can have a profound impact on various aspects of our lives, including our mental and physical health and family dynamics. From overflowing closets to disorganized living spaces, stuff can create a chaotic environment that affects our overall well-being. However, by taking easy steps toward organizing, you can experience the joy and serenity that comes with a sparse space.

When you're surrounded by stuff, you might feel anxious or stressed. Just knowing you have all these items around you can feel overwhelming. Even if you want to clean, there's so much around you that you don't know where to start. This will weigh on your mind and make it hard for you to relax and find peace, even though your home should be your safe haven. You might feel mentally exhausted as your mind struggles to eliminate all the external stimuli in a space and allow you to focus on one thing.

Conversely, when your space is clean and organized, you feel calm and relaxed. You can move around your home without bumping into things and can find what you need without searching endlessly. Since your mind doesn't have all the visual distractions of stuff, you can focus easily. These factors all work together to reduce your stress levels. When you feel less anxious, your body and mind feel freer, and you'll notice a boost in your productivity and creativity.

However, not everyone feels negatively toward the stuff around them. Some people are perfectionists and don't like seeing things piled up around them, while others may feel cozy and protected when they're surrounded by all their belongings (Fuller, 2022). I've helped many people who collect items that others may deem "clutter," like leftover fabric pieces, cotton, broken crockery, and piles of magazines. I would always wonder, even as a kid, what purpose these items served. Later in life, I realized that they served more of an emotional need than a practical function.

As individuals, we have to assess and decide what each item means to us. It comes down to understanding why people keep things and being empathetic. Sometimes, it's an emotional attachment to things that loved ones gave them, and they want to keep the memories close. Other times, it's because they feel prepared when they have everything around them. I've known several artists who want to keep their paints nearby, jumbled, so they'll have them handy when inspiration strikes and generally find that inspiration strikes when things are a mess, not neatly aligned. Some people may feel like their possessions are important because they show what they can afford, so they want to have more and more things around them. Others may wish they could declutter because they don't care much for their possessions but are afraid of change. The idea of having a clean home may appeal to them, but the idea of changing their house and lifestyle can seem daunting or scary, so they keep living their lifestyle instead of pushing beyond their comfort levels (Orr et al., 2017). This book does not sit in judgment of anyone who finds solace and comfort in their stuff. If you recognize the need for help in removing stuff, then this book is here to assist you in your journey.

Living in a crowded space can also impact your family dynamics. When you're surrounded by stuff, you can't find what you need. You may accuse someone in your home of taking or misplacing an item when it's just hidden among your stuff. Living in a clean, organized house provides a home base for harmony and cooperation that you'll feel reflected in your personal relationships.

A mess can also impact you physically. If you have too many things in your home, you'll have trouble moving around. Stacks in the hallways can narrow the space even further, and you can even trip over items in the room. Having too much stuff in your home means they'll accumulate dust, which can negatively impact respiratory issues and make it difficult to truly clean your living space. If you're surrounded by things, you may not feel inspired to get up and move around, so you become acclimated to a sedentary lifestyle, which can be detrimental to your physical health.

With fewer items around you, you'll feel more productive and creative because you don't have to spend time and energy looking for things or cleaning. You'll feel proud of your accomplishment because you're living with things you need and use. Knowing your home is clean and efficient will make you feel calm and serene, which boosts your mental well-being.

While I've found that decluttering has a positive impact on my mental health, there isn't a specific science I can quote that proves this outcome. I'm not writing this book as a claim to cure mental health issues, but rather to share my personal strategies for organizing and feeling happier and freer.

Discover Joy in a Clutter-Free Space

You can discover joy in a clutter-free space beyond feeling proud of your organizational accomplishment. In this process, you're creating a sanctuary where you and your loved ones can thrive. You'll approach this activity from a place of mindfulness so you're aware of what you're doing and why, every step of the way. That level of involvement makes it easier to maintain your ideal styles of organization and minimalism. Intentional cleaning helps you prioritize your values and ensures your home reflects what you love and respect.

When you've completed the first step of decluttering, you'll find yourself motivated to continue because of the joy you find in your new living situation. You'll feel gratitude for the layout of your home and how you've displayed your meaningful possessions in ways you can constantly appreciate them. Aesthetically pleasing and purposeful items contribute to an atmosphere of happiness and contentment, so without the surrounding stuff, you'll find joy in your space.

You can share this joy by inviting friends and loved ones into your refreshed home. You'll have space for larger gatherings and can enjoy your time spent with others instead of worrying about your belongings or how your belongings might impact their opinion of you. In that way, you'll realize how organizing allows you to let go of many things that are holding you back—both physical items and emotional connections to your belongings.

A Little About My Journey

My name is Zohra Mutabanna, née Zohra Mubeena. I grew up in Bangalore, India. Every summer, I visited my dadi (paternal grandmother; pronounced daa-dee) who lived in the old city of Madras, now called Chennai. I loved spending time there to the extent that my parents let me live with her for an entire year! During that time, my dadi would let me have free reign in her house. She had so many treasures that I always found something fascinating. I would rummage through her cupboard drawers and find knick-knacks like beaded dangling earrings, perfume bottles with a lingering scent, shiny chains, scraps of stunning fabric, and ink pots stained with all colors. My grandmother let me keep my favorite treasures in a small box that I'd quickly fill to the brim! However, once I got home, I would have to narrow down my treasures to only a few; otherwise, my small box wouldn't have room for more treasures. I had to inspect each item and spend time thinking about what I wanted to keep and why. That was my first lesson on letting things go, and it stuck with me throughout my life.

When I was instructed to pick what to keep and what to give or throw away, it brought forth many conflicting feelings, especially since I was still a young girl—it was a mixed bag. I could always decide what to keep but found it harder to give things away. In those moments, my mom urged me to ask myself why I wanted to keep something, what I intended to do with it, or how I could think of regifting it, if the item was a piece of jewelry, for example. Obviously, a lot of things didn't make sense, but with a small house and four siblings sharing the space, we all had to compromise. Being the oldest, the stakes were high sometimes because I had to be a role model. With encouragement and support from my parents, I learned to navigate some hard times. Now, when I look back, I realize that it was a lesson in empathy. Sometimes, my items were thrown away without my knowledge and it broke my heart. I promised myself that when I grew up and had my own kids, I would never throw away my kids' stuff without their permission. Of course, as a parent, I think differently today. I will admit that I have thrown away stuff that my kids would probably think of as treasure when they were little. But as they have matured, I have taken a step back to let them decide. Giving stuff away is never easy; it's a journey. What may be "stuff" to someone may be "treasure" to another. As I write this book, I acknowledge that identifying clutter may vary from person to person. If you identify something as clutter, then my hope is that this book will help you address it at your own pace and time.

In 2000, my husband and I set out to move to a new continent. Moving is already expensive, but shipping things overseas is so exorbitant that we knew we had to think carefully about what to take. I thought of my dadi and knew I would be able to let things go and only move what mattered most to us. Over the years, my husband and I naturally started living a minimalist life, which was helpful when we needed to move quickly for work or to save money on rent. As a child, I thought living a spartan life would be uncomfortable because I'd miss so many comforts of a cozy, crowded home. However, I've come to love our lean living space because that means we have even more room to fill with our love.

We've lived this way for over two decades, and I can't imagine going back to an overstuffed space. We have adolescent children and, while any parent will tell you that kids come with things, they've naturally picked up our lifestyle and share the same values about what is worth keeping and what they can let go.

How This Book Will Help

Over time, so many friends have reached out to me to help them organize that I knew having a written guidebook would help others exponentially. While I'm not an expert, I have over 20 years of experience in organizing and maintaining a minimalist lifestyle, so the methods you'll read about are tried and true.

This book goes beyond telling you how to tidy up—it includes checklists for each area of your home and effective strategies for letting go of things you keep out of obligation or sentimentality. I've found that releasing possessions doesn't mean you eliminate the emotional connection you had with an object or the person who gave it to you, but it rather helps you appreciate that bond in a new way.

You'll learn how to set your intentions and follow through to reach your goals. Steps for organizing and cleaning will ensure your house stays pristine even years after you start the major process. The book ends with information on changing your mindset and lifestyle to naturally promote a minimalist life. A holistic approach to organizing allows you to fully understand how this process not only cleans your home but also reduces stress and increases your happiness.

With all that said, what are we waiting for? Let's get started!

Chapter 1:

Your Decluttering Journey

Clutter is nothing more than postponed decisions. –Barbara Hemphill

Decluttering is a broad process. Knowing how to get started will help you figure out a plan and decide how you're going to approach the mess. I love having goals and plans because if I ever feel stuck, I can just refer to my notes and take the next step to ensure I don't lose momentum. Whenever I feel like I don't know where to start, I remind myself that habits in motion are habits in action, and make a move.

Make Space for What You Need

It's always easier to do nothing than to do something, so start with nothing. Picture your home as a clean, organized place that helps you feel at peace. Even if you don't know what action to take to get there, you can see that picture in your mind and feel inspired to do something—even if it's the one-minute cleanup!

Just by picturing a clean house, you'll get an idea of what goals you can set. Look at your entryway and determine what needs to go. Maybe the space isn't really big enough for a side table and hooks. You can choose to only hang a few items in that space and move the side table somewhere else to stack your mail. Or better yet, handle the mail as soon as you bring it inside so it doesn't have time to accumulate!

Turn this critical eye on every area of your house. Envision how you want the area to look, as this will help you understand what you need to get rid of. You can then make notes about how to achieve that goal. For example, you can recycle magazines from the coffee table and shelve the books you left there to have a clear surface in the living room. This is a small goal that you can easily mark off your list after just a few minutes of work. Eventually, establish a routine of putting away books and magazines after you read them, instead of letting them stack up on the table.

Some people I help think they don't need lists and priorities, but I always suggest this step. Skipping it might make you feel like you're able to jump right into cleaning, but before long, most people are treading water because they're unsure what to do next to achieve their dream minimalist aesthetic. A broad goal for an organized home isn't always enough to ensure you can make progress.

A general goal is to clean your house, but you should be specific. Do you want to give away items you don't use or store them for six months? Do you want to keep sentimental items or strive to break those emotional attachments? Do you want to store documents in a filing cabinet or keep digital copies on a hard drive? With questions like this, you can see how one broad goal actually breaks down into multiple steps that give you a clearer path to progress.

Beyond the goal of a minimalist home is your priority for each room. Do you want to keep your living room cozy and comfortable with throw cushions but have your bedroom sparse and organized? Understanding your vision for each area of your house can help you determine a plan of action instead of sweeping through every room and following the same steps, even if you're not trying to achieve the same goals.

I recommend prioritizing areas with the most mess. Many people prefer to start with their closets. You look at your clothes every day as you pick your outfit. You open the closet to put away your laundry. Cleaning up this area first can help you feel more in control of your possessions. Having a sparse closet will make it easier for you to see what you have, put away your belongings, and feel motivated to achieve that same goal in other areas of your home.

The pantry is a similar area that is relatively easy to clean and organize. Go through your food items and get rid of expired goods. Put the newest items at the back and move the older ones to the front so you'll use them before they go bad. Once you finish your pantry, you can organically move on to the kitchen cabinets or refrigerator to keep the momentum and continue cleaning one of the most important rooms in your home.

I've found that an agile mindset helps tremendously, not only with decluttering but also with being proactive and efficient in running my household. An agile mindset comes from the idea of the growth mindset, proposed by Dr. Carol Dweck in her book *Mindset: The New Psychology of Success* (2006). It's a technology framework that can be applied to our daily lives. This framework proposes the ability to adapt and adjust, upon introspection, if something isn't working. In the context of organizing things, it enables you to

- pace yourself as needed.
- take small steps and not feel overwhelmed.
- create realistic and doable goals.
- celebrate small successes (the concept of rewarding can be tied to this).
- not overcommit—the one-minute clean-up, for example.
- reflect and make changes.

A growth mindset means that you're open to new ideas and are a lifelong learner. When you hit a roadblock in your life, you don't get discouraged—you learn what you need to know to overcome that obstacle and move on. With a growth mindset, you think outside the box and get creative with your approaches to life and problem-solving.

An agile mindset puts you on the path to a growth mindset because it allows you to be malleable (Sloan, 2015). Cleaning and organization are not a sprint but a marathon that requires pacing and adjusting for positive outcomes. You may try one method and if it doesn't work, you either refine the approach or try something new. An agile mindset prioritizes responding to change so you aren't stuck in a rut.

Having an agile mindset has helped every aspect of my life. It can help you at this stage of sorting because, after you set goals, you need to think innovatively to know how to approach them. It will also help you manage stuff in the future and be more efficient with your housekeeping. I previously mentioned an approach to organizing your pantry and refrigerator where you put the items you need to use up-front and push back items with a longer shelf life so you can use things before they go bad. To add to this approach, I also keep a magnetic whiteboard on the refrigerator door. When I'm low on or out of an item, I write it on the whiteboard. Since I go to different grocery stores for specialty items, I always keep two columns on my board. If I need a third, I just add it to the bottom right. When I have three columns, there's one for "Organic", "Specialty", and "Bulk/One-off" items. That way I have a dedicated space to write what I need from each store. When I go to the store, I get everything I need without first needing to make time to take stock of my kitchen. Writing down what I need as I run out of it takes just a few extra seconds but saves me so much time in the long run.

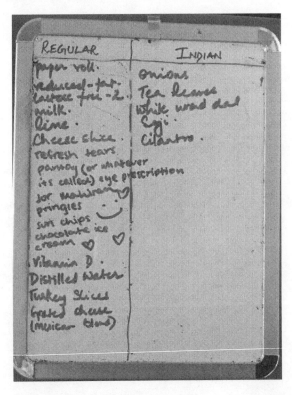

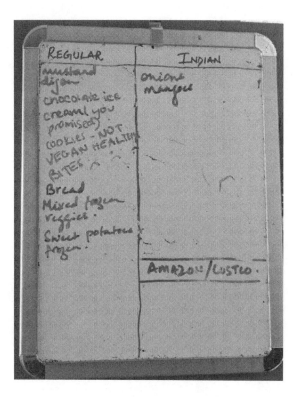

As you can see, one thing about using a whiteboard is that anyone can write on it! I'll add necessities for the meals I plan for the family, then my teenagers will follow behind me and add what they want. Clearly, they hold me to my word and never forget when I promise a treat, like ice cream! And if I try to counteract that sugar with healthy sweets, they call me out—"Cookies, not vegan health bites!" It's hard to keep junk out of the house with teens around, but I must say, with these hungry, growing kids, the junk isn't here for long! It's one of those battles I'm slowly conceding as if decluttering my mind! I'm sure other parents can relate.

I used to keep a magnetized pad of paper on my fridge and a piece of paper taped to the inside of my pantry door. I'd write dry goods on the pantry list and other items on the fridge list, but I wouldn't always remember to grab both pieces of paper before I went to the store, so I'd only know what refrigerated items I needed and not dry goods, or vice versa. Then, I started writing what I needed on slips of paper as soon as I thought of it. I quickly realized I would have five papers in different rooms of the house. If I managed to get them all to the grocery store, it would be a miracle! My agile mindset helped me realize that paper is too easy for me to misplace or mistake as trash. Writing on the whiteboard keeps the items in my sight and I can simply take a photo of the board before I go shopping. No paper, no extra time, maximum efficiency!

With all these approaches to setting goals and trying to streamline your life, it's easy to get lost in the details. Because of that, I advise people to reward themselves after achieving each goal. Once you clean the kitchen, maybe you can treat yourself to dinner at your favorite restaurant. After you clean your bedroom closet, you can kick back and watch a few extra episodes of your favorite show. When you clean out your bathroom cabinets, you can use some of the items you find to pamper yourself with an at-home spa day. Think of something that you really want so you feel motivated to reach the goal and enjoy the reward.

Assess Your Clutter

Once you have your broad goal and some smaller goals based on room or time restrictions, you can dive deeper and start to assess your stuff. Some people have tons of paper—mail, magazines, coupons, and takeout menus—stacked around their homes. Others might have more clothes than they need. Some people have collections that take up a lot of space, and even more people have the general mess that accumulates over time, like assortments of kitchen goods, cutlery, sets of dishes, winter accessories like scarves and gloves, and miscellaneous items that somehow move with you from home to home.

When you assess your belongings, you start getting an idea of what to do with them even before you take action. For example, people with paper piles can recycle takeout menus because the information is available online. They can recycle old magazines or upcycle them for crafting projects. They can ensure their coupons aren't expired and keep them handy (in their wallet or with their grocery list). They can scan or photograph important documents and save them on the computer or file them in a lockbox to prevent loss due to fire.

Though the paper approach may seem very straightforward, you can apply it to any type of clutter. Just as you envisioned your sparse home as your final goal, look at each space in your home and assess the mess that is clouding its basic style. What is in front of your walls and windows? What is on your furniture? This is clutter. Even if it's items you want to keep, like your sweater tossed on the back of your couch, it counts when it's not in the right place. Assessing will show you what you can get rid of and what you need to put in its place before you even make a move! The best part of the first two stages of decluttering is that they are mental tasks that you can complete while sitting and checking out your house. You won't have to stand up and move things around until you're ready to get started, meaning you can conserve your energy for the physical act of cleaning and maximize your efficiency.

Categorizing your belongings before you start the process helps. Think about broad categories like clothes, books, electronics, sentimental items, and kitchenware. As you sort them, you'll see how much of each category you have compared to what you actually need. This will help you decide if you need to eliminate items in a specific category to curb stuff. However, remember that you're still just assessing and getting an idea of what you have and what you need at this stage. This legwork will help you create a plan of action.

Create a Plan of Action

After all this assessment, you most likely have a plan of action in mind. Writing your plan down is the best way to ensure you can feel in control of the process. This also helps people who are neurodivergent, such as those with ADHD, or people who are so busy they have trouble focusing on one specific task or dedicating time to it. When you have a written plan, you'll know exactly what you need to do every step of the way, whether you have one minute to clean or one hour. In fact, having an assortment of short-term and long-term goals on your list will ensure you can always take action, no matter what other commitments you're juggling.

I prefer to create a plan of action by looking at my goals and writing each one at the bottom of its own sheet of paper. You can also do this on a whiteboard or an app on your phone, but I like seeing it written out because I can then keep the papers on my desk until I'm ready to clean. This way, I can take papers referencing my bedroom items to the bedroom and mark off tasks until I finish. This way I won't have to constantly go back to another room to look at the whiteboard or won't get distracted by other apps and alerts on my phone when I just need to see what's next. I use this method for almost everything in my life. I keep a to-do list of notes and tasks for my podcast, *Inside Tech Comm with Zohra Mutabanna* (created under my married name). I have another for my role as chair of my kids' school PTA. When I have tasks that don't need to be done right away, I enter them into my phone, leave notes, and set a due date. It might seem like a lot of work, but it helps me stay on track and prevents me from forgetting things that might otherwise slip through the cracks.

After writing the goal at the bottom of the paper, I go to the top of the sheet and write down small steps I can take to reach that goal. I leave room in the margins for my timeline and to check off each task when I complete it. For some lists, like those that deal with my wardrobe, I never write a timeline. I generally try on a few extra garments when I have time and donate or sell them if they don't fit or suit my style anymore. For other lists, like anything dealing with a mess in high-traffic areas like the kitchen or living room, I give myself a week or so to accomplish all the tasks.

While some tasks don't have a timeline, I always give myself a *time limit*. This makes my decisions quick and permanent. When I try on a garment from my closet and it doesn't fit, I don't give myself time to look at it and think, "Well, I could strive to lose weight," or "Maybe a tailor could take in the waist a bit." I tell myself it doesn't fit and immediately discard it to donate or sell. I never give myself more than a minute to decide. If you don't immediately know if you need to keep something, you don't need it. When you find an item that is a necessity, you have that answer right away. I look at my warmest winter coat and know I'm keeping it. For my lightweight jacket, I give myself a minute to think about how often I wear it with our seasons so quickly transitioning from warm to cold and know it's not worth the space it takes up in my closet—quick, easy answer that I won't backtrack on.

Gather Supplies

The supplies you need for decluttering will vary depending on your method. For example, the four-box method requires—you guessed it—four boxes! I actually prefer to use boxes for many cleaning approaches simply because they're easy to store or take to donation centers when it's time. I also keep a trash bag handy for trash I encounter as I clean, as well as items that are beyond repair. Some people like to have storage containers and organizers handy so they can put things away as they sort them, so this might be an option for you. If you don't want to use that approach, you can put things in a box to sort or store later.

I like to keep a pad of paper and marker handy so I can add stuff to my list or, better yet, mark things off! The marker is also ideal for labeling boxes if I need to document exactly what I packed inside. I also keep my paper lists nearby when I'm working in certain areas so I can track my progress.

Depending on how much time I have to work, I also have cleaning supplies ready. It's nice to clear off my dresser and dust the surface while I'm already there. Too often putting off the cleaning part of the process means it won't happen for weeks, and you'll end up living in a dusty home until you make time to clean.

If you have a lot of paper, keep a shredder handy. If you don't have one, you might be able to rent one from an office supply store or find a place that will shred documents for you. This is safer than recycling important documents because it obscures your personal information and makes papers impossible to put back together, keeping your identity secure.

If you clean whenever you have time, keep a timer handy or set an alarm on your watch or phone. You may think that the task is tiresome, but it's easy to get carried away once you get started and lose track of time before you know it! Timing yourself ensures you don't spend too much time on one area and stay efficient with your progress.

While it's not exactly a supply, I recommend you have music, podcasts, or audiobooks playing while you work. It's nice to have some background noise and sometimes the distraction of music or voices can help you make quick decisions because you work without focusing too much on each belonging you touch.

Sort Your Belongings

Our lives are filled with a multitude of possessions, ranging from sentimental items to everyday necessities. Over time, these belongings accumulate and create chaos within our living spaces. Sorting through them allows you to assess what truly matters and make informed decisions about what to keep, donate, or discard.

Sorting has numerous benefits. Primarily, it helps you create a clear and organized living environment. This can lead to reduced stress and anxiety because a neat space fosters a sense of peace and calm within you. Additionally, sorting through your belongings allows you to rediscover forgotten treasures, reconnect with cherished memories, and let go of things that no longer serve a purpose in your life. I can't tell you how many people are amazed at what they find when I help them sort and organize. They'll encounter things they forgot about or items they've searched for but were unable to find! I like to call it a treasure hunt not only because you might find things you appreciate but forgot about, but also because taking stock of your belongings and striving to clean each area of your home is the true treasure.

Before embarking on the sorting process, gather some essential supplies such as storage boxes, trash bags, labeling materials, cleaning supplies, and a notepad or your phone to jot down notes and reminders. Having these items on hand will make the sorting process more efficient and manageable. You won't have to get up and go grab something, which can interrupt your flow and make it more difficult to get back in the right mindset to organize.

Depending on how much stuff is in your home, sorting through your belongings can be a time-consuming task. Allocate sufficient time to avoid rushing the process. Find a designated space where you can lay out your belongings and sort through them comfortably. This could be a spare room, a large table, or even your living room floor. When you can see everything at once, you'll have a better idea of what you want to keep and what you can get rid of. For example, if you lay out your clothes and realize you have four black tops, you can easily choose three of them to donate because you know you'll still have one to wear. While laying everything out takes up space, it will save time!

You can also sort your belongings before you lay them out in groups. Seeing the items several times may help you take stock of them: as you gather them from wherever they cause a mess, as you group them with similar items, and as you lay them out to see the big picture. Some ways you can group them include

- essential daily use items
- essential non-daily use items
- sentimental items
- unused or unwanted items
- broken or damaged items

If you follow those guidelines within each room, you'll break the belongings down into manageable groups to sort further. For example, in the bathroom, you'll have a group of essentials like your toothbrush and paste, hygiene items, toiletries, and makeup. Items you don't use daily may include cleaning products or beauty treatments you use monthly or seasonally. Expired medications and old makeup would count as damaged.

I recommend that beginners try the quick decision method of Keep, Donate, and Discard, which you'll learn more about in the next section. But before you reach that stage, you can look at each item as you sort it and think about its usefulness and sentimental value. Ask yourself if the item still serves a purpose in your life or if it makes you happy. If it doesn't, consider donating or selling it to someone who may find value in it. For sentimental items, focus on keeping the ones that truly hold significance and memories.

Decide What to Keep, Donate, or Discard

Deciding what to keep, discard, or donate is a crucial step in the process of organizing your belongings. It involves making thoughtful decisions about each item, considering its usefulness, sentimental value, and impact on your life. Knowing what factors to consider when you decide what to keep, donate, or discard will make the process much easier for you. You'll also get ideas on how to discard, donate, or sell items responsibly.

Keep

When deciding what to keep, consider the following factors:

- **Usefulness.** Practical items are worth saving, especially if you use them often. Keep your favorite outfits, kitchenware you use often, your daily toiletries, and items relating to your passions and hobbies.

- **Multiples.** If you have duplicate items, you can safely earmark the extras for donation or sale because you know you'll still have one of what you need.

- **Space Constraints.** Houses get messy because they don't have endless space. Think of where you can keep belongings, whether on display or in storage before you commit to keeping them.

- **Sentimental Value.** You don't need to discard things that mean a lot to you just because you want to live in a sparse home. I always recommend that people find unique ways to display sentimental items, like hanging a grandparent's ornamental plate or putting keepsakes on the edge of the bookshelf. If you don't have space to display them, consider keeping one storage box of all your sentimental items so you have them, but they're not in the way.

- **Future Need.** There's no reason to discard items you don't use daily if you use them sometimes. I keep holiday decorations even though I rotate them and only use each once a year. It's more efficient to store them than buy new ones annually. Similarly, you might have tools or devices you don't use often, but it's better to have them on hand when you need them!

Donate

Donating or selling your items can be very fulfilling. You know that items you don't use anymore will go to someone who needs them. Selling items also helps put a bit of money back in your pocket while ensuring they have found a good home. That said, you should choose items that you yourself would get instead of offloading everything you don't want, regardless of their condition.

Items you donate or sell should be in good condition. If the item is dirty or dusty, clean it before donation or listing it for sale. If it involves damaged fabric, repair it first. You wouldn't want to receive or buy a dress with a hole at the hem, so don't give things away in that condition.

Research charities in your area to see where you want to take your donations. Some charities mark up donated items and make a profit.

Others give the items to people who truly need them at no cost. Charities and nonprofits also have distinct missions and values, so find one that aligns with your beliefs.

You can also donate items to people you know. I've had people compliment my clothes or accessories, so when I'm ready to get rid of them, I offer them to those friends first. I know they'll appreciate them and that makes it worth it to me.

Consider the value of the item before you earmark it for donation or sale. Unless you plan to have a big garage sale, it might not be worth selling smaller items at a lower cost. If you sell things online, you should consider the value of your time as you photograph and list the item. Doing all that for something that will sell for a few dollars is rarely worth the effort.

Discard

When you're ready to discard things, use the following ideas to decide what to get rid of.

- **Broken Items.** Items that are broken and unable to be repaired can go into the trash. If you have broken items you intend to repair, be honest with yourself and your timeline. Will you repair it and use it within the next week? If not, it's only creating a mess.

- **Missing Pieces.** Everyone has random pieces they hold on to because they're sure that, one day, they'll find what it belongs to. Or, conversely, they have board games with lost parts. If you can't play the game without those pieces, you can discard it or list it online as a game for parts—someone may find what they need from your offering! But there's no reason to hold on to small parts or incomplete objects because you don't know that you'll ever find the missing pieces, so you're holding on to useless items.

- **Outdated Technology.** It's hard to let go of technological devices because, in most cases, you spent a lot of money on them, and they were once top-of-the-line. But if they're outdated or can't perform their functions, you should discard them. This includes phones, computers, gaming consoles, and software you don't or can't use anymore.

- **Expired Products.** You shouldn't keep expired products like food, medication, makeup, or toiletries. Dispose of these items to eliminate the mess. Follow my previous tips to organize perishable items to ensure they don't expire before you can use them.

Before you toss items in the trash, consider what they contain and dispose of them properly. Some locations ask you to take technological devices to a specific recycling center. If you have old paint cans, pesticides, or cleaning solutions, you may have to take them to a hazardous waste site instead of throwing them in your trash can. Always sort out discarded items that can be recycled too.

Assess Sentimental Items

Sentimental items often hold strong emotional value, making them challenging to handle during the decluttering process. When you sort your belongings, keep all sentimental items together. You don't have to go through them immediately or even in the same cleaning session. You may need more time to assess the items and determine how much they mean to you. I always recommend doing a cleaning session and, while you're in that same mindset, going through a few sentimental items. You'll be primed to get rid of stuff so you're more likely to be honest with yourself about what you actually need to keep. But it's also a nice way to wind down after doing a lot of work.

The decluttering process is different for sentimental belongings. The item might not be useful in your daily life, but it still matters to you. Be honest about both aspects to determine if something is worth keeping.

Sentimental items may include photos of people you love or important experiences from your past, heirlooms handed down through your family, or thoughtful gifts from loved ones who are no longer with you. It's hard to part with these items because of what they represent. You can remember people and events without holding on to physical reminders. I always recommend people journal their memories associated with each item, as it helps them recapture every moment of that person or event. You can also take a photo of the item and attach it to the journal page so you have the visual and the memory without needing a physical item taking up space.

Most people keep sentimental items because of guilt or obligation. They feel bad getting rid of something their grandmother made for them or a loved one gifted them, even if they don't need or use it. You shouldn't let these feelings of obligation make you keep things that don't bring you joy and only create a mess.

If you're unsure about your memories or reason for keeping items, consider taking photos of them. You can put the image files on your computer or a small external hard drive and not keep the physical items around anymore. Another way to keep a few special belongings is to give yourself one storage box. You can keep any items that fit in the box while still allowing the lid to close. Once your box is full, you can't keep more sentimental items unless you get rid of something already inside.

Instead of discarding sentimental items, you can also feel better by donating them either to another family member, a charity, or a related nonprofit. Some people who have family heirlooms can donate the items to local museums to add to exhibits. Or maybe your cousin has always loved a painting your grandmother gave you, so you can pass it on to her instead. Just ensure you're making wise choices instead of burdening someone else with your items!

Chapter 2:

Organizing

Your home is living space, not storage space. –Francine Jay

While decluttering can seem like a daunting task, especially when confronted with years of accumulated belongings, effective organization plays a vital role in making this process more manageable and rewarding. Organizing during cleaning is not just about neatly arranging possessions; it's a strategic approach that brings clarity, order, and harmony into our lives. Whether you're decluttering your home, office, or any other space, the key to success lies in establishing a systematic method for sorting, categorizing, and storing items. A well-organized environment not only looks aesthetically pleasing but also has numerous benefits for your mental well-being and productivity. Once you have an organizational system in place, you'll find that it's easier than ever to keep your minimalist life calm and peaceful. Your solid foundation will inspire you to clean up after yourself as you go about your day instead of letting it sit and putting in more effort later. Remember, habits in motion are habits in action, so organizing your space will help you develop strong habits.

Create a Designated Place for Everything

In the quest for a minimalist and organized living space, one of the fundamental steps is to create a designated place for everything. An orderly home or workspace not only enhances efficiency but also brings a sense of peace and tranquility. By assigning specific spots for items, we can easily locate what we need when we need it, reducing stress and saving valuable time. With that in mind, this section explores the art of organizing every corner of your home, including the kitchen pantry, bedroom closet, and bathroom cabinets. You'll learn practical ways to maximize storage, minimize stuff, and streamline your daily routines.

Kitchen and Pantry Organization

The kitchen is the heart of the home and keeping it organized is essential for a smooth cooking experience. By creating a well-organized space, you'll be able to find ingredients and cooking utensils easily, minimize food waste, and keep your kitchen looking tidy and inviting.

Of course, you'll need to start by discarding expired food and broken items from the kitchen and pantry. Donate kitchen gadgets you don't use so you see what you have left and how much space you have for storage. Group similar items together to create categories. For example, place all baking supplies in one area, group spices together, and keep canned goods in a separate section.

Arrange things so you can easily access them to streamline your cooking process: store frequently used items within easy reach, keep everyday dishes, glasses, and utensils in accessible cabinets or drawers, and store lesser-used items higher up or at the back of shelves.

Transfer dry goods like flour, sugar, pasta, and grains into clear, airtight containers. This method not only keeps them fresh but also allows you to see the quantity at a glance, making it easier to add them to your whiteboard grocery list when needed. Labeling containers and shelves can be a game-changer in maintaining an organized kitchen. Use labels to indicate the contents of containers and identify where each category belongs.

To make the most of your kitchen space, use shelf dividers and organizers in the cabinets and pantry. If you have deep shelves, I recommend installing risers so you have two shelves on each opening and can see the back items above those in front. You can also install hooks or racks on the inside of cabinet doors to hang small items like measuring spoons, pot holders, or small cutting boards. Over-the-door organizers for pantries can give you extra storage space.

For your drawers, organizers are key. They will keep your forks, spoons, knives, and other utensils from getting jumbled together, and you'll know exactly where to look when you need a specific cooking utensil. I know some people who love the look of a jar on the counter with their large wooden spoons and serving utensils, but unless your kitchen style is homey, I recommend keeping those items in a drawer so your counters are clear. Sparse counters will naturally inspire you to eliminate clutter in other areas. I suggest that you only keep essential appliances and frequently used items on the counter. However, you can also look into efficient options, like microwaves you can install over the range, as they double as an overhead vent and free up your counter space.

Bedroom and Closet Organization

Bedrooms should be a sanctuary for rest and relaxation and free from chaos. When your room is clean, you'll feel prepared for quality sleep every night because you won't see piles of stuff waiting to be put away. It's also easier to find the clothing and accessories you need in the morning so you're not stressed and rushing before you even start your day. With that goal in mind, keep your bedroom clean and closet organized.

As you assess your belongings, get rid of things you don't wear or that no longer fit. Then, separate your clothing into categories, such as shirts, pants, dresses, and so on. This will make it easier to organize and find specific items when needed. You'll see what you have left and can determine how much storage space you need, which will help you decide on how you want to organize your items.

You can maximize closet space by using double-hanging rods to utilize vertical space effectively. Using the same type of hanger throughout your closet creates a visually pleasing and organized look. Slim, non-slip hangers are a great choice as they save space and keep clothes from slipping off. If you have enough storage space, consider rotating your clothes based on the season. Store out-of-season clothes in boxes or under-bed storage to free up closet space for items you currently wear.

Install shelves or drawers to store folded clothes, bags, and accessories. You can also add hooks to the inside of the closet doors to hang scarves, belts, or hats. Use clear storage containers or bins to store shoes, accessories, or special occasion clothing so you can see what's inside but do label the containers for easy identification. Shoe racks or shoe shelves help keep your footwear organized and easily accessible. A shoe organizer that hangs over the closet door or on the wall will save floor space and can keep everything in your closet so your bedroom remains minimalist.

Many people automatically leave things on flat surfaces. If you have this issue, I recommend limiting the number of side tables, dressers, and cabinets in your home. That said, a dresser and nightstand in the bedroom are ideal for additional storage space, so you may want these pieces. If you use them, keep them clean. Your dresser can store undergarments, socks, accessories, and smaller clothing items you can fold, but make sure you put things away in the drawers instead of letting anything pile up on the flat surface. For your nightstand, you should only keep the essentials out: a lamp, alarm clock, and maybe a book you read before bed. Once you finish that book, put it away instead of stacking your new book on top of it. Many nightstands include storage space below, so keep that organized if it's open. If yours has a drawer, keep it clean. Even though it's out of sight, you'll see the mess when you open the drawer, and that can impact your calm state of mind before you go to sleep.

Bathroom and Laundry Room Organization

The bath and laundry rooms are often small spaces, but with strategic organization, they can become functional and efficient.

In the bathroom, start by going through the cabinets, drawers, and shelves. Dispose of expired medications, old cosmetics, and unused or empty containers. Keep only things you use daily or regularly. Group similar items together and store them in containers or baskets. Limit the number of items you keep on the bathroom countertop, only keeping the essentials, like hand soap and toothbrush holder. You can store occasionally used items in higher or less accessible spaces.

Use dividers and organizers in your bathroom drawers to keep toiletries, cosmetics, and grooming tools neat and easily accessible. Transfer cotton balls, cotton swabs, and other small items into clear containers to keep them visible and organized. If you have the space, install shelves or wall-mounted cabinets to make use of vertical space to store towels, extra toiletries, and other bathroom essentials. You can also add hooks or towel racks to keep towels and robes off the floor and easily accessible. This helps maintain a clean and organized appearance in the bathroom, and you can find things without having to rifle through a pile of items.

Use a similar approach for the laundry room, as these rooms are usually small and contain the same type of things you might not use daily but still need to keep on hand.

Keep laundry supplies like detergent, fabric softener, and stain removers organized by storing them in bins or on shelves. Categorize laundry items for easy access. If your space allows, install shelves or cabinets in your laundry room to store laundry baskets, cleaning supplies, and other household items. Label the containers to make it easy to identify each item and prevent mix-ups. If you keep other tools like mops, brooms, and ironing boards in your laundry room, hooks and wall organizers can provide more space.

If possible, dedicate a flat surface, such as a countertop or table, as a folding station for freshly laundered clothes. You can also install a hanging rod or retractable clothesline for air-drying delicate clothing or hanging shirts right after ironing. You'll be able to complete every aspect of your laundry routine in this organized space. With that in mind, consider integrating a regular laundry routine. That will keep dirty clothes from piling up, and you'll go into the room often and can maintain the same level of organization without a mess forming.

Living Room Organization

The living room is where we entertain guests and spend quality time with family, so it must be tidy and organized. A well-organized living room not only enhances the overall aesthetics of your home but also creates an environment that promotes comfort and harmony.

As always, begin by removing items that don't belong, especially those that have wandered into the living room from other areas of the house. Divide the living room into functional zones, such as seating areas, entertainment zones, and reading corners. Position furniture in a way that promotes conversation and creates a natural flow in the room. Avoid blocking pathways and ensure that seating is accessible and comfortable.

I recommend seeking out storage furniture like coffee tables with shelves or drawers, ottomans with hidden storage, or media consoles with cabinets. These pieces help keep the living room organized by providing a designated spot for items like remote controls, magazines, and board games. You'll have everything you need in the room, but it will be tucked away, keeping the room visually pleasing.

Another way to help with this mess is to designate a focal point in the living room, such as a fireplace, TV, or a piece of art. Arrange furniture around this focal point to create a cohesive and visually appealing space. Use that as your center and decorate thoughtfully without overwhelming the room with too much art, especially art that doesn't work well to bring the room together.

Use shelves and bookcases to display decorative items and store books, photo albums, and other cherished possessions. Arrange items aesthetically and avoid overcrowding. Place decorative baskets or bins in the living room to corral small items like throw blankets, toys, or magazines. This keeps items organized while adding to the room's decor.

Designate a specific spot for electronic devices like remote controls and chargers to prevent them from getting misplaced. You can then conceal cords and cables from electronic devices using cord organizers or cord covers. This will help reduce visual distractions and create a cleaner look in the living room.

Along with regular tidying up, consider changing and rotating decorative items according to seasons or special occasions to keep your living room fresh and interesting. I like using seasonally attractive blankets and pillows to make the room look nice. That way, every season the room looks new without needing to buy new items. I rotate the blankets and pillows before my family gets tired of looking at them, so it always seems bright and inviting.

Home Office and Study Space Organization

Whether you work from home or need a designated area to study, an organized space fosters productivity and focus. A well-organized home office allows you to find what you need easily, reduces distractions, and enhances creativity.

By now, you know to start: Assess your home office space and remove any items that you no longer need, such as old papers, outdated office supplies, or broken equipment. Divide your home office into functional zones based on the type of work you do. For example, you may have a zone for computer work, a zone for writing, and a zone for storage.

Keep your desk tidy and sparse. Use desk organizers, trays, and holders to store pens, notepads, and other frequently used items. Set up a filing system for important documents and papers. Use folders or filing cabinets to keep everything organized and easily accessible. Put labels on drawers, containers, and shelves to quickly identify the contents and make it easy to put things away when you're done. Set up an inbox tray for incoming documents and an outbox tray for items that need to be dealt with or filed. Regularly go through these trays to keep them from overflowing.

Organize your digital files on your computer or cloud storage. Create folders and subfolders to categorize documents for easy retrieval. After losing information from an old hard drive that became unreadable, I was a cloud storage convert! My favorite thing about this method is that you can access your data from anywhere. If I'm visiting friends and want to show them a specific picture, I can just pull it up on the cloud using my phone or one of their devices instead of needing my external drive. However, the best option is to use several storage methods. Keep documents on your computer, a backup drive, and in the cloud if possible. That way you have multiple options in case of failure and won't lose your information.

Utilize vertical storage options like shelves, cabinets, and wall-mounted organizers to maximize space and keep items off the floor. Many people think that office storage only includes desk drawers, filing cabinets, and bookshelves. But I've seen effective organizers that include cubes you can hang on the wall over your desk and shelves in every shape and size, so you're sure to find some that will suit your workplace and give you plenty of storage without compromising on your style.

Furthermore, to feel comfortable in this space, ensure your desk and chair are set up ergonomically to support good posture and reduce strain on your body during long periods of work. I also recommend a standing desk. I use one every other hour to prevent myself from sitting on a desk chair for too long. Also consider adding personal touches like motivational quotes, pictures, or plants to create a pleasant and inspiring workspace—but not so much that it looks clunky!

Sentimental Collections

Organizing sentimental collections can be both challenging and rewarding. Sentimental items hold emotional value, so you must handle them with care and respect. Begin by assessing your sentimental collection and curating it to include only the most meaningful items. Let go of duplicates or items that no longer hold strong sentimental value.

Group similar sentimental items together based on themes or relationships. For example, you can create categories for family mementos, travel souvenirs, or childhood memories. Decide how you want to display your sentimental items. Options include shadow boxes, display shelves, glass cabinets, or dedicated memory boxes. Choose a method that suits the items and your available space.

Some sentimental items may be delicate and prone to damage. Invest in proper preservation materials, such as acid-free tissue paper, archival boxes, or protective sleeves, to ensure longevity. Consider digitizing sentimental items that are prone to wear or deterioration. Scan photographs, letters, or other paper-based items, and create a digital archive to preserve the memories.

Label each item with information like the date, location, and significance. Keeping a journal or digital document detailing the stories behind each piece can add depth to your sentimental collection. It can also help your family members understand why you kept certain items and whom they remind you of, thus giving them a chance to learn more about you and their history. I want to admit that this is one area that I have been working on for some time. It hasn't been easy, so I've tried to break it down by events or memories—for example, my wedding album: I'm going through each picture, and then writing down the names of those in the picture before my memory fails me. I'm trying to employ my agile mindset here in that I try to do things in small increments and then revisit what worked or didn't work the last time. This helps me stay motivated, but like everything else, it's a journey for me.

Personal Photo Collections

Organizing a personal collection of photos is a great way to preserve memories and make it easy to find specific pictures when you want to revisit them. Collect all your physical and digital photos from different sources—old photo albums, shoeboxes, memory cards, cameras, smartphones, and computers.

For digital photos, delete duplicates, blurry images, and poor-quality pictures. Be selective and keep only those that hold sentimental value and create folders to categorize them. Some common categories could include "Family," "Vacations," "Events," "Friends," etc. Create subfolders within each category for more specific groupings. Give your photo files descriptive names that help you identify the contents at a glance. For example, "Family_Christmas_2019" or "Vacation_Italy_2021." If you have physical photos or printed albums, consider digitizing them using a scanner or a scanning service. This will help you incorporate them into your digital photo collection.

It's crucial to back up your photo collection regularly to prevent loss due to computer crashes or accidental deletion. Use external hard drives, cloud storage, or both for added security. You may also want to print photo books for special events and as a quick, easy way to share copies of photos with family and friends. You can make affordable, hardback photo books online and store them on your bookshelf, instead of bulky photo albums or loose printed pictures.

Use Storage Solutions and Organization Systems

Storage solutions and organization systems come in various forms, catering to different needs and spaces. These solutions are designed to help you maximize storage capacity, reduce mess, and maintain an organized environment.

Shelves and cabinets are versatile storage options that can be used in almost any room. While wall-mounted shelves are great for displaying items and keeping them off the floor, cabinets with doors are ideal for concealing items and maintaining a clean look.

Bins and baskets are excellent to organize small items like toys, office supplies, or toiletries. They can be placed on shelves or in closets to create designated spots for specific categories of items. You can also hide these containers away by using those that fit under your bed or other furniture. Such low-profile under-bed containers are great for utilizing unused space to store items like clothing, bedding, or seasonal gear.

Drawers provide hidden storage and are commonly found in dressers, desks, and kitchen cabinets. Drawer dividers are useful to keep items separated and organized.

Closet organization systems are customizable solutions that include various components like shelves, hanging rods, drawers, and shoe racks. They help optimize closet space and keep clothing and accessories neatly arranged. You can also include over-the-door organizers, which are ideal for storing shoes, cleaning supplies, or accessories without taking up floor space.

Wall organizers come in different designs and can be used to store and display items like mail, keys, and office supplies. They are perfect for small spaces and entryways. Other types of wall organizers are pegboards and slatwalls. They feature hooks and holders you can adjust to accommodate various items, making them highly customizable for tool storage, craft supplies, or garage organization.

How to Choose an Organizational System

Before selecting a storage solution, assess what items need organizing and the specific requirements of your space. Consider the type of items you need to store, the available space, and any specific design preferences you may have. You might want something that offers the most storage behind cabinet doors or a unit that matches your decor. Think about how often you'll need to access the items. If they are frequently used, opt for solutions that provide easy access, like open shelves or bins. Look for storage systems that offer flexibility and customization options. Adjustable shelves, movable dividers, and modular components allow you to adapt the system as your needs change.

Accurate measurements are essential to ensure that the storage solution fits the available space perfectly. Take measurements of height, width, and depth to find the right fit.

Determine your budget before starting your search. Storage solutions are available for various budgets, so plan accordingly.

Before making a final decision, read reviews and testimonials from other users to gain insights into the unit's performance and durability. Many people include information in their reviews about what they store and how they enjoy the product, so you'll get a clearer picture of how the unit may help you.

Maximize Space and Efficiency

Maximizing space and efficiency is key to creating an organized and functional home. Implementing smart strategies and optimizing storage solutions can help make the most of your space while also increasing overall efficiency. The units mentioned above give you an idea of how you can make the most of your space, especially by hanging things on walls to maximize vertical space. Storage furniture is another great way to make the most of the space you have. You know you'll have a couch in the living room, so why not choose one with storage space in the armrests for remote controls, books, and other items that would otherwise be strewn on a table?

For efficiency, regularly sort and purge items you no longer need or use. This prevents unnecessary items from taking up valuable space and makes organizing more efficient. Labeling everything also helps you keep track of what you have and how much. I also recommend the "one in, one out rule," meaning if you bring something home, you need to get rid of something you already have. That way, instead of bringing in more items, you're keeping your house at the same level of minimalism, just with new objects instead of the same old stuff.

As you clean your home and introduce organizational systems into your lifestyle, you'll learn natural ways to be clean and efficient thanks to your agile mindset.

Chapter 3:

Cleaning and Maintenance

Less stuff means less to clean, less to organize, less to store, less mess. −Unknown

Once you declutter your home, you might feel like you're done. However, you still need to take action to keep your space clean and maintain your ideal level of organization. Being proactive about maintenance will ensure you don't have to deep clean your house again in the near future. The tips in this chapter will help you develop a strategy and put those habits in motion to become habits in action.

Establish a Cleaning Routine

A well-structured cleaning routine is crucial for maintaining a clean and organized home. Breaking down tasks into manageable chunks and assigning them specific frequencies helps efficiently tackle cleaning duties and prevent an overwhelming mess. You can choose to clean daily, weekly, or monthly and delegate certain tasks to specific times to best manage your schedule and keep your house looking amazing. The following schedule is just a jumping-off point; you'll find what works best for you as you start developing a routine.

Daily Cleaning

In the kitchen, wipe down your counters and tabletops daily and wash the dishes and sweep the floor after meals.

Ensure to also wipe down surfaces in your bathroom to keep them clean and prevent mold buildup in your bathtub or shower.

For frequently used living areas, clean up each day and dispose of or put the items where they need to go. Make sure things look tidy and inviting by folding afghans on your couch and fluffing pillows.

Your bedroom cleaning routine will depend on your style. I recommend making your bed every morning because it pulls the room together and makes it look tidy instead of disheveled. However, if you don't want to spend time on that task, ensure you prevent stuff from accumulating on your nightstand or dresser and hang clothes that are on the floor, furniture, or bed.

You can determine what tasks you'll do daily based on what you see around your home at the end of each day. You might just want to quickly tidy up the main rooms of your home, perhaps spending a bit more time in the kitchen to keep things clean.

Weekly Cleaning

In the kitchen, clean the oven and stove top, sanitize the sink, and mop the floors. Take stock of what you have in the fridge and pantry and add items to your grocery list. When you return from the store, unload the items and put them away immediately so they don't crowd your counters. Remember to arrange things properly so you don't forget about them and can use them before they expire.

In the bathroom, clean the shower walls and tub, wipe the mirrors so they sparkle, and clean the toilet. You'll also want to change the towels and put away dirty items in the laundry.

For bedrooms, a quick vacuum and dusting should do the trick. Also, change your bed linens and put away the dirty ones in the laundry.

After you do the laundry, tidy up the laundry room by putting away all your supplies and wiping down the appliances. Remember to also clear out the dryer lint trap for cleanliness and safety. Take the clothes to the designated bedrooms and put them away immediately, hanging them or folding them into drawers instead of heaping them on the bed for later.

Dust your other rooms and then vacuum or mop your living areas to clean up the debris you dislodged. You can also clean the windows to ensure the sunlight brightens your space.

Weekly cleaning requires a little more effort than daily cleaning, but you can still take time on the weekend to look around your house and see what you can put away quickly to maintain your ideal level of cleanliness.

Monthly Cleaning

While monthly cleaning takes a bit more work, with your daily and weekly cleaning adding up, you won't actually have much to do beyond regular maintenance.

In the kitchen, you should sort out the pantry: move items that are about to expire to the front of the shelves so you can use them for next month's meal planning. You can also deep clean your oven, microwave, refrigerator, and other appliances.

In the bedrooms, rotate and flip the mattresses. Clean under the bed to catch anything that might have gotten pushed beneath. Check the closets to ensure no mess has built up there. Go through your drawers to see that everything is still sorted and folded.

In the living areas, vacuum your furniture and wash the throw pillows. Dust ceiling fans and wipe down baseboards to give the house a pristine appearance. If you have blinds on your windows, clean those either by dusting or taking them down and hosing them off outside. You can also take down your curtains and wash them.

After completing daily and weekly cleaning, you'll have a good idea of what you'll need to add to your list for monthly maintenance. Check if any of these larger tasks can be broken down into smaller weekly tasks to lighten your workload.

Seasonal Cleaning

Some people don't do seasonal cleaning if they stay on top of their other routines, but I recommend it if you change your home decor seasonally. If you decorate your house for seasons or holidays, set aside some time for this every season. You can change throw pillows and blankets in your living room seasonally as well, so having a separate cleaning routine for this can help.

If you change your wardrobe based on the weather, a seasonal clean is ideal for your closets and dresser drawers. For example, you can rotate out your winter jackets and only wear sweaters as winter turns to spring, and then put away your sweaters and get out warm weather clothes for summer.

I like to defrost my freezer during spring and fall cleaning, but once a year is enough if you don't see much ice buildup inside. If you've neglected your ceiling fans and light fixtures during the other cleaning routines, tackling them seasonally is a clever alternative. You may also want to thoroughly clean your carpets beyond the usual vacuuming.

Prevent Clutter From Building Up

Stuff can quickly take over our living spaces, leading to stress and disorganization. By adopting simple yet effective strategies, you can prevent clutter from accumulating and maintain a tidy and organized home.

One In, One Out

As mentioned in Chapter 2, the best way to prevent a mess from building up is the "one in, one out" rule. If you bring something home, get rid of something else. That way, you know you're not bringing in so many items that you don't have room to store them all. When you follow this concept, you'll automatically pause before you buy something new and think about how much you truly need it. Basically, once you've organized your home, you know you have everything you need. So, if you bring home something else, you'll have to get rid of something that survived your initial purge, which implies it's something you need or love. While you might know what you can give away to welcome this new item into your home (and that's fine!), you might also realize that you don't really need it, thus saving money and preventing clutter in one fell swoop.

Paper Pile

Another aspect to look into when clearing out stuff is your paperwork. It's easy to let this pile up because it takes many pages before papers start to seem like a mess. However, most paperwork is important, so if you have everything in a stack, you won't find what you need. Go through all your paperwork and sort it into folders or envelopes and easily tuck them away in a desk, file cabinet, or even a storage box in a closet. This way, you'll know what you have and where it is, so you can locate important documents easily. Just make sure they're important! Avoid storing junk mail, takeout menus, or paperwork that you already have in your email or backed up to a drive or the cloud. If you clip coupons, use them before they expire, or recycle them if you don't end up using them. Shred paper to ensure no one can get your personal information and do this organization and shredding as soon as you bring paperwork into the house instead of letting it accumulate.

All Hands on Deck

To prevent stuff from building up, encourage everyone in your house to put their things away after use and clean up daily and weekly along with you. Often, it falls on one person to sort the entire house, but that can be a lot of work. You may also not know what someone wants to keep, so you risk discarding too much and throwing out things they wanted. My friend used to tell her daughter, "You better clean this room or I'm putting everything into garbage bags!" That would get her daughter moving, but a lot of her stuff went under the bed or in the closet.

Tackle the initial steps of decluttering with your children to help them understand what needs to be done. It took some time with my kids, but once they learned it, they had no problem following along. Now I know they're actually cleaning their rooms instead of just hiding the mess. If you feel like you'll be nagging your family to put their things away, just mention it in a kind voice, implement a "clean as you go" policy for the house, and lead by example. When they see how easily you organize and how nice the house looks as a result, they'll feel inspired to do the same.

Tips for Keeping Your Home Tidy and Organized

If you're looking for quick fixes, this section contains tips collated from the rest of the book that will help keep your home tidy and organized. I've put together all of it in one place so it's easy to dog-ear this information.

- **Use storage solutions.** Containers, shelves, and cabinets help keep things organized and out of sight so your house looks tidy. You can also find furniture with built-in storage, hang shelves on your walls, and utilize over-door organizers. Keep in mind that you don't need to go to a store and purchase these items, as that can be expensive. Look around your house to see what you already own but don't use and repurpose it for storage. You can also look for cheap items at dollar stores, find free stuff at flea markets, or check neighborhood apps for giveaways and affordable yard sales.

- **Get rid of everything you don't need or love.** Having less in your home makes decluttering that much easier. Once you clean, be thoughtful about what you bring back into your home. Adopting a minimalist mindset and following the "one in, one out" rule greatly helps you stay proactive against a potential mess.

- **Go digital!** Consider digitizing photos and documents so you can keep things in the cloud or on a small external drive instead of keeping cumbersome photo albums and stacks of paperwork in your home.

- **Make time to clean.** As you learned in Chapter 1, you don't need an hour to clean every day. You can accomplish a lot in a minute, so take advantage of your free time to tackle your belongings before they escalate into a mess.

- **Designate a space for everything.** If you have a hook for your keys and an inbox for your mail, you'll put things where they belong instead of leaving them around on random surfaces—you'll also easily be able to find anything you need quickly. Earmarking space for everything will ensure everyone in your house can help you keep it organized.

- **Follow a cleaning schedule.** With regular cleaning, you're not overwhelmed at once and you can keep your house fresh and polished. You'll also know what you need to do and when without letting dirt and your belongings pile up.

Chapter 4:

Mindset and Lifestyle

Owning less is better than organizing more. –Joshua Becker

Many people think the act of decluttering is enough—you'll have a clean house and can live happily ever after. However, by now you know that a certain level of continuous maintenance is required to keep things tidy. That's why changing your mindset and lifestyle can really help keep your house organized—it will also keep you happier and healthier!

The Connection Between Clutter and Mental Health

The state of our living environment, particularly the presence of too much stuff, has a profound impact on our mental well-being. Numerous studies have explored the relationship between clutter and mental health, shedding light on how a disorganized space can affect our emotions, cognitive function, and overall sense of well-being.

In some cases, you may want to organize your house but a family member could be struggling with it. Instead of pushing ahead with the process I've shared in this book, I suggest pausing and talking with them. Show empathy and let them know that you're willing to hear their side of things. Brainstorm ways you can help them organize their space and let them shop with you for storage solutions. When they're part of the process, they'll feel more involved and empowered and can help in a way that's comfortable for them.

Some studies have found that women who think they live in an overcrowded home have higher cortisol levels than others, meaning their stress levels are higher (Rogers & Hart, 2021). You may feel overwhelmed when you look at your surroundings, which can make everything seem chaotic, causing a mental overload.

Having a lot of stuff around can also distract you. You have so much to look at that you can't focus on one thing, which makes it hard for you to think clearly. This goes hand-in-hand with how belongings can make you procrastinate (Lauster et al., 2016). If you have so much around you, you don't know what to do first. Keeping everything organized shows you exactly what you need to do without the distraction of piles of belongings around you.

Moreover, mess can negatively impact your relationships, which can be detrimental to your mental health. If you want to be organized and your spouse, family members, or roommates have too many belongings in the common areas, or they don't clean up after themselves, you might resent them or feel negatively toward them. If you live in a messy home, you might not want to invite people over because you feel embarrassed by your belongings or don't have space for everyone to gather. This lack of social togetherness can negatively impact your relationships and your mental well-being, making you feel isolated.

A messy house can also lower your quality of life in many other ways. You may look at your surroundings and feel frustrated that you let things pile up, while still not knowing where or how to start. You may also struggle to do your daily tasks because you have to move stuff off your counter to prepare dinner or search for clean clothes from those piled on your bed. With a minimalist home, you can eliminate all that frustration and time spent searching to instead be with your loved ones, participate in your hobbies, or relax and enjoy your space.

Creating a Clutter-Free Lifestyle

Given all the signs of mess being detrimental to mental health, it's understandable how the KonMari method of only keeping things that bring you joy became such a popular way to downsize. While that's one option, there are actually many ways you can create a minimalist lifestyle.

You should address decluttering by making a conscious effort to address your problem areas. For example, you may think stuff accumulates due to incoming mail or doing laundry, but the core issue may be that you let catalogs pile up and bring home new clothes every time you go shopping. Now that you've identified the root of your problem as buying new items when you already have everything you need, you can start clearing up knowing that you just need to take stock of what you own and appreciate it. In this scenario, you could reorganize your closet, bring little-worn items into your wardrobe rotation, and recycle catalogs as soon as you get them in the mail instead of keeping them around to flip through and find something you want.

With this example in mind, you can embrace the principles of minimalism and get rid of what you don't need by appreciating what you have. Thus, by shifting your focus from the material possessions you own to the relationships you have with others and the experiences you have in life, you can live more intentionally. With a minimalist home, you'll feel like you have more time, energy, and mental space to fully engage with these people and experiences.

The right mindset and proactive approach to a minimalist lifestyle will make your work easier than ever. You'll understand that you can discard, donate, or sell items you don't need and know that people who need them will receive them and put them to good use. You can start with small areas to prevent feeling overwhelmed, and as soon as you see your progress, you're sure to feel inspired to continue, either going through each room or tackling similar categories of belongings.

Tips to Stay Organized and Minimize Future Clutter

As I constantly tell myself—and now you!—habits in motion are habits in action. These tips will help you stay organized and develop minimalist habits so you won't bring more items into your home.

1. Be mindful of how you spend your money and what you bring into your home. Always think about whether you truly need an item before you buy it. Avoid impulse purchases that seem like a good idea and give you a buyer's high but generally end up unused.

2. Develop a routine that helps you keep your home clean without allowing stuff to build up. Seeing too much to do can make you shut down and feel like you'll never make a difference.

3. Consider scheduling your cleaning tasks. Pick a specific day for laundry, one for pantry organization and grocery shopping, and another for bathroom cleaning. You'll know what you need to do each day without letting one area of your home get out of control.

4. Declutter regularly. While this book gives you the steps to tackle your first deep dive, you can use the process over and over! You might not need to deep clean every time, but it can help to refresh your approach periodically. For example, if more kitchenware or clothing has accumulated, or if you have some things you stopped using or wearing since your last deep dive, you can donate them to others.

5. Try storage solutions. Even if you start living a minimalist lifestyle, you might want new ways to organize your belongings or keep them out of sight. I always recommend under-the-bed and over-the-door storage options as ways to keep things nearby without causing a mess. You don't even have to buy flashy organizers from stores—use things around your house,

like baskets and bins, or repurpose items into storage options, like keeping pens in a mug or glass.

6. Ask for help. Everyone at home should be on board with keeping things looking as nice as possible. Lead by example but let them know that everyone benefits from a beautiful, organized home, so they should all chip in and not let too much work fall on one person.

One thing I've found helpful is to take my favorite tips and cleaning routines and put them on a chart. I've known people who use similar chore charts for their children as they grow up because the visual element helps people remember what they need to do each day, not to mention the sense of satisfaction in marking things off! You can have fun with it and use cute stickers to identify tasks you've completed. When you fill in your chart, reward yourself with a nice dinner, day of relaxation, or fun experience out on the town.

This chore chart came from a dear friend who made it for her young daughter. You can follow this template of morning and evening chores or use this type of heading for different rooms in your house. You can highlight the specific days on which you do things that aren't daily tasks. For example, if the first heading is "Kitchen," you can include duties like "Wash the Dishes," "Wipe the Oven," "Clean the Fridge," and "Mop*." You'll wash dishes daily, but you may only need to highlight the Saturday square for wiping the oven and cleaning the fridge. The asterisk (*) next to mopping can remind you that this is a monthly task.

There are many ways to make this type of chart work for you, so consider adapting it to your needs to streamline your decluttering process!

Chapter 5:

A Quick Review of Popular Decluttering Methods

Decluttering is infinitely easier when you think of it as deciding what to keep, rather than decide what to throw away. –Francine Jay

I have intuitively used some of these concepts in the earlier chapters, but these specific methods are available to you for further reading and discovery. One of the biggest roadblocks people encounter when decluttering is that there are many different approaches. You may have heard a lot about the KonMari method from Marie Kondo's best-selling book and Netflix show, but that doesn't mean it's right for you. Many methods can help you organize, and finding the right one can make all the difference in the effectiveness of your goal to clean and keep a sparse home. We'll review some of the most popular methods to see which one works for you.

As you read over these methods, think of how you like to manage your home. Some people love to do a few minutes of cleaning every day to ensure their home stays tidy. Others may prefer to deep clean every weekend to prepare their space for the coming week. As long as you pick an approach that is realistic and won't overwhelm you, you'll streamline the organization process. You can always try an option and if it doesn't work for you, shift to another approach. Over time, I've pulled elements from several of these methods to cobble together my own cleaning style, focused on my mantra, "Habits in motion are habits in action." Let's get into these cleaning concepts and see what resonates with you.

The 5S Method

This method is typically used for workplaces, but I've found it effective for home use as well. The 5S concept comes from the Japanese words Seiri, Seiton, Seiso, Seiketsu, and Shitsuke, which translate to Sort, Set, Shine, Standardize, and Sustain (Fallon, 2023). While the idea comes from the automotive industry, its practicality made it a favorite approach for home organizing as well. The terms themselves give you an outline of how to go about the process.

- **Sort:** Go through your belongings and determine what to keep, what to donate, what to sell, and what to throw away.

- **Set:** Take your most used items and make them accessible yet organized and out of the way.

- **Shine:** Keep all your items, the room, and your house clean and functional.

- **Standardize:** Develop a routine for this process so it's easier to continue doing over time.

- **Sustain:** Follow your routine daily, weekly, monthly, and seasonally—whenever you feel the need to better organize your home.

One of my favorite things about the 5S method is that it outlines the entire process for you, so it's ideal for beginners. You won't feel overwhelmed as you look around your home because the first S tells you exactly how to start. You know that you need to assess your belongings and keep only what you need. If you find yourself getting stuck in the sorting process, I recommend using this method in a room like the kitchen, where all items have specific purposes and it's easier to identify what you need, what you use, and what is taking up space. In your bedroom or living room, where you have seasonal items or sentimental items, this approach might be too cut-and-dried for you.

The One-Minute Rule

Some people decide to organize their homes and directly jump in but quickly tire themselves out. Regardless of how much time you carve out to clean or how you limit yourself in terms of the room or space you're working on, the process can take a lot of energy and emotional willpower, so many people prefer to start small. The one-minute rule is the best way to get into cleaning if you're worried about wearing yourself out or biting off more than you can chew. It will also help if you don't have much time to dedicate solely to organizing. Instead of procrastinating for one day when you envision you can spend hours cleaning, start now with one minute.

Yes, you really only need one minute for this process! It's not just a catchy name. You need to think of tasks that take a minute or less to complete. I've found that this approach is a great way to change daily habits. For example, instead of taking off your shoes as soon as you come into the house and leaving your bag on the floor, tuck your shoes under the entryway bench or put them in your closet. Hang your bag by the door or in your bedroom. There! You've already made your space look nicer without leaving stuff behind. After you do this for several days, you'll find that you naturally start putting stuff away instead of cleaning up after yourself.

While the concept behind the one-minute rule is to do small cleaning tasks as you have time, it also conditions you to take care of things right away instead of letting them hang over your head. So many people take stock of their homes or cars and see the accumulation of trash and belongings that wouldn't be there if they had cleaned up along the way. Taking time to proactively clean up after yourself can change your habits and, in turn, make that one minute of cleaning even more powerful! You won't need to dedicate hours to cleaning your home because you've taken care of the little things.

What I love about the one-minute rule is that it applies to everything! I use it to reply to emails and pay bills as well. As soon as I get a new message or have a bill come in, I reply or pay it right away so it's off my plate. Otherwise, I risk telling myself, "I'll get to that later," and then forgetting or having it hang over my head and taking away focus from other things.

The Four-Box Method

The four-box method is similar to the 5S approach in that it tells you exactly what to do! Find four boxes (or storage bins, bags, or even group things in piles—don't let the word "box" keep you from getting started!) and label them as Trash, Give Away, Storage, and Put Away.

The Trash Box

The Trash box should be for things you don't want anymore but aren't in good enough shape to donate or sell. Clothes damaged beyond repair are trash because you don't want to donate those to the less fortunate—just be honest that no one will wear them! However, you can always consider reusing worn clothing as rags. I have a bin of fabric scraps like old socks, parts of torn skirts, and t-shirts with holes that I'll use to clean the house until they're about to disintegrate—*that's* when they're truly trash! But if you won't use that type of thing for rags, it's better to be honest and throw them away first thing instead of letting them stick around and crowd your space.

The Give Away Box

The Give Away box should contain things that other people can use. You may want to donate these things to charities in your area or pass them along to friends who'd use them. You can also consider selling them at a garage sale to get a bit of pocket money. Everything in this box should be in decent condition, like clothes that still look great but you just don't wear or working electronics you don't need anymore. If you can mend clothes, make sure you actually have the time to do so before keeping items that may just make a mess and adding tasks to your to-do list. Consider troubleshooting electronics that don't seem to work or list them online for people to use as parts to repair their items.

The Storage Box

The Storage box will keep items that you don't want to get rid of but don't use in your daily life. This can include seasonal clothing and holiday decorations. Consider keeping several storage boxes in different sizes so you can group things together. I keep all my winter clothes in one clothing box, and when I move them to my closet, my summer clothes go into that clothing box for maximum efficiency. However, I also have boxes for holiday decorations, clearly labeled so I can store them according to when I'll need them. I also keep tools, like supplies for hanging artwork, tucked away in a box with other home improvement tools. I don't need them often, but when I need them, I want immediate access to get the job done. It's not worth getting rid of these items and re-buying them when I need them, so storage works best.

The Put Away Box

The Put Away box is for items you use daily. As previously mentioned, you may come home and take off your shoes and bag, leaving them near the door. You may take off your jewelry and put it on the table beside the couch today, but tomorrow you'll put it on the kitchen counter. When you go to clean these rooms, you'll find items that you use so often, you know they should have their own space. Keep shoes on the floor of your closet, hang your bag on a hook over the door, and put a small bowl on your dresser to collect jewelry. Now when you find items during your cleaning, you'll have places to put them. If you start putting items in this box that you don't use often or don't have a designated spot, think honestly about how often you use them and if they're worth keeping. You might want to find a dedicated storage space for them to prevent mess.

You can use the four-box method for each room to prevent feeling overwhelmed. While you can throw away trash and put away other items, it's best to stockpile your storage and give away boxes until you have enough contents to organize your storage containers, donate to charities, or set up a garage sale. Whatever you do, keep the items out of sight so you're not tempted to rifle through the boxes if you start to have doubts! Once you make a choice about an item, that should be your final decision. If you let yourself think that you might need to keep things, you'll be back at square one.

The Six-Month Policy

The six-month policy is a great way to clean your house if you're unsure of what you should keep and what you don't need anymore. Some people struggle with items because they think, "What if I need it in the future?" Indeed, you don't want to get rid of something just to find yourself buying it again weeks later—it's a waste of money and resources. It's also an easy way to discourage yourself from decluttering because you'll tell yourself, "I *knew* I should have kept that!" and will resist getting rid of other items.

The six-month policy is simple: Whatever you haven't used in the past six months is something you don't need anymore. The obvious exceptions are holiday decorations, sentimental items, and seasonal wardrobes.

You can approach this in several different ways. Some people can go into a room, especially the kitchen, and think of when they last used an item. As I mentioned at the beginning of this book, many people will buy kitchen devices, use them once or twice, and put them away. They know they haven't used the rice cooker because it's dusty, or because they remember the last meal they made with it.

Some people can't remember dates like that. In that case, you might want to box up items you haven't used within your recent memory and tuck them out of sight. Write the date on it. After six months, if you haven't gone into the box to find a necessary item, you know you can sell or donate all of them.

You can adapt this method for clothing too. When I hang my seasonal clothes, I try to wear every item at least once. If it doesn't fit well or doesn't suit my style anymore, I put it in a six-month box to assess later. That way I don't have to worry about my clothing piling up while I easily clean other belongings with this method.

The six-month policy isn't a harsh way to declutter. You can give yourself grace by allowing decorations, knick-knacks, and sentimental items to stay (Use a different approach to get rid of those if you think you have too much). You can also reflect on items by asking yourself why you haven't used them in six months. Was it something you needed but couldn't borrow from a friend, so you had to buy it yourself? Was it an impulse purchase? Did you intend to use it often but forgot about it? You can always give yourself time to use the item—put it in a visible place and think about it whenever you're doing a task it could help with. If you still don't find yourself using it, you know you can get rid of it without regret. This thoughtful approach can help you assess why you buy items, which can eliminate clutter before it comes through your door!

The KonMari Method

Marie Kondo and her KonMari method recently took the decluttering world by storm. It goes above and beyond an organizational approach as it's more of a lifestyle shift. The basic concept of the KonMari method is that you keep items that bring you joy. Not only will that help you eliminate unnecessary stuff, but you'll also be surrounded by belongings that make you happy for a win-win approach to cleaning!

This approach takes time and consideration, so it's best to try when you don't have a deadline and can think about your belongings as you work. Instead of solely organizing, this method is more about keeping items you love and use. Since you most likely don't feel attached to every item in your home, you'll get rid of things by default and have less to organize and clean. It's an ongoing approach, so you'll have to go through your things periodically—annually or seasonally. This process is special because it involves going through your belongings and feeling joy from what you choose to keep.

It's best to approach things by category instead of location for the KonMari method. Go through all your clothes, whether they hang in the closet, remain folded in the dresser, or are packed away in seasonal boxes. Sort through all your clothing at once so you know what you have and can make the right choices about what brings you joy. Marie Kondo recommends starting with your clothes because they often have less sentimental attachment than other items, so you'll get a feel for the method without too much of a struggle. Then you can move on to other possessions, like books, kitchenware, paperwork, and miscellaneous items.

The first step of this method is to discard what you don't need or what doesn't bring you joy. The next is to organize what remains and clean the mess. Kondo's approach favors simplicity, meaning you keep all your rain gear in one closet, instead of keeping the raincoat near the door, boots in your bedroom closet, and umbrella by the back door. Keeping similar items together makes them easier to find and helps you know what you have instead of feeling like you need to buy something new to fix a need.

The Danshari Method

The Danshari method of decluttering comes from Fumio Sasaki, author of *Goodbye, Things: On Minimalist Living*. The three Japanese characters that make up the term "Danshari" translate to refuse, dispose, and separate (カミラ [Camilla], 2018). It also includes concepts relating to yoga and Buddhism, inspiring people to also engage in disposing of mental and emotional burdens along with physical items.

The overall concept of Danshari is that less is more. It's a minimalist lifestyle focused on Zen. The goal is to live a deliberate, mindful life of simplicity so you can focus on what truly matters instead of being attached to materialistic goods.

As you might expect, the three Japanese characters outline the process of this method.

Refuse

Refuse is the first step because you work against bringing more items into your home and refuse to let your belongings define you. This refusal means you're restricting mess and turning your back on the acceptance of a consumerist society. You acknowledge that you don't need possessions to enjoy your life and show your worth. You don't need to spend money on physical goods to feel complete—you're refusing to participate in that aspect of society.

Dispose

The second step is to dispose, which is more action-oriented than refusing. You assess your belongings and sort them, disposing of things you don't need. It's especially helpful to launch into this part after the refusal stage because you've adapted your mindset toward shopping, consumerism, and owning things, so you feel less attachment to your stuff.

Separate

The third step of the process is to separate. In this case, separation means you sever your attachment to your physical belongings. It's rooted in a Buddhist concept of non-attachment. When you don't feel bonded to your belongings, you'll be happier with less and experience less stress. You can devote more energy and attention to your loved ones, your health, your passions, and traveling. Think about what you value and realize that you'll be able to prioritize your interests over seeking pleasure from physical goods.

That may sound like the exact opposite of the KonMari method, which tells you to keep things that bring you joy. However, you can still appreciate your belongings and feel joy when you're surrounded by them! You just don't tie that joy or appreciation to your sense of self-worth. If you lose an item, you don't feel discouraged or upset—you feel separate enough to shrug it off and continue moving on with the things that matter most to you.

The Furoshiki Method

The Furoshiki method is a beautiful, eco-friendly way of decluttering and eliminating waste. It's a way to wrap and carry items in cloth instead of needing disposable bags, containers, and packaging. Your items will look much more appealing in fabric wrapping than in a plastic grocery store bag, and you can use the fabric over and over again. This is also a great way to wrap gifts, especially for those people who like to carefully open gifts and save the paper and bows for reuse. Unlike paper and plastic, which deteriorate over time, fabric will last much longer!

You can find Furoshiki cloth, which is typically cotton, nylon, silk, or rayon, in many sizes. Choose smaller cuts of fabric to wrap the lunch you take to work but a larger cut for a big gift or to pack items for a vacation. You can also use fabrics you already have. I mentioned reusing clothing for rags earlier, but you could also use it as Furoshiki cloth. If you have t-shirts with holes in the armpit, you can cut off the top of the shirt and undo the side seam to have a bit of fabric for wrapping. Similarly, unravel skirt seams to get a lot of fabric on hand. You can also buy fabric from craft stores and hem the edges to prevent fraying.

This approach to packing and storing is very eco-friendly because you're not using plastic bags and containers. You don't need to buy gift wrapping paper, which often has a slick coating, making it difficult to recycle. It's also easier to wrap things with fabric instead of searching for the right size of box or container, especially for gifts that might have irregular shapes. When you wrap things in fabric, you have all the supplies on hand! You can knot the fabric around the items instead of needing scissors to cut the paper and tape to hold the ends in place.

Back home, in India, my mom still wraps clothes in small bundles called *potla* (poht-la). She uses cotton or linen fabrics that belonged to my grandmother to wrap her seasonal clothing. While fancier styles are replacing this timeless and environment-friendly option, you will still find a few *potlas* in my house—my wedding dress, for instance, is wrapped in *potla* fabric that my nani (naa-nee; maternal grandmother) gave me. It's surprising how long-lasting these simple storage strategies can be!

If you want to be even more eco-friendly, use Furoshiki cloth until it wears out, or if you don't need it anymore, use the fabric as rags or to wrap items you need to store away and not access often. This approach is much better than using plastic bags or containers, or even cardboard boxes, which use a lot of resources for creation and recycling.

I have a few more tips that tie in more with eco-friendliness than specifically the Furoshiki method, but while you're thinking of how to incorporate cloth wrappings into your daily life, these ideas will keep you on the right track. I have been using nylon and fabric grocery bags for over a decade now. My husband and I always keep bags on hand or in our cars to reduce plastic use. Some stores even charge for plastic or paper sacks now, so this way you save money and always have your bags on hand to reuse. It has become a lifestyle choice for us. Beyond that, my kids carry stainless cutlery to school for lunch instead of using plastic options that cost money and will be thrown away after a single use.

Also, I carry empty plastic containers with me when we go to a restaurant. That way, I can bring leftovers home instead of using a new container. This is not easy to do all the time, but I always try to reduce wastage. Just being mindful is half the battle won. Over time, it becomes easier to implement, as you hear in my mantra "Habits in motion are habits in action." Small acts like this, along with the Furoshiki method, contribute to an eco-friendly lifestyle that will come naturally to you in time.

The Swedish Death Cleaning

Margareta Magnusson wrote the book *The Gentle Art of Swedish Death Cleaning: How to Free Yourself and Your Family from a Lifetime of Clutter* as a way to help people remove unnecessary belongings from their homes. As the title implies, it's recommended for people who feel closer to the end of their lives, but no one knows when they'll die, so it's worth using this in-depth approach to improve your home while you're still able to enjoy it!

The concept comes from the idea of your loved ones having to clean out your home after you pass away. I've heard so many stories of people who go through their parents' belongings and have no idea why they kept certain things. It takes a lot of time to clean out a house, and when you're already grieving someone, it can be a very difficult undertaking. By practicing Swedish Death Cleaning while you're still alive, you're taking stock of everything you have and making the cleaning process easier for anyone you leave behind.

Contrary to what some people have gone through after losing their parents, my mom has given away everything that she owned. She truly lives a minimalist lifestyle. She chose to give away what she has in her lifetime to her children. I take deep inspiration from this. Her mother was like this too. My mom is almost 80 today, and her material belongings would fit inside a small suitcase. She is happier with so few belongings so she can focus on family and friends. And she knows that when she passes away, she won't seem like a burden to us in terms of cleaning out her home. It's an inspirational way to live, though you might want to follow some of the other decluttering methods here as you work your way up to my mother's level of commitment!

Since death cleaning is such an involved task, Magnusson's book covers sentimental items and personal mementos. Instead of feeling sad as you follow this approach, you'll appreciate everything you have and think about why you kept them for so long, which can be a great time for reflection.

The approach has you start with simple tasks—the bigger the better! For example, look at your furniture. Do you need a table in the kitchen and another to create a separate dining area? What about armchairs and side tables? These large items crowd your open space and are impersonal, so they're easy to get rid of and show you what a difference death cleaning can make. Then move on to clothing, books, and other belongings before spending time with personal items like photographs and letters.

While the objective of decluttering is always to get rid of things, with death cleaning, you may want to keep things for your loved ones. Maybe you spend time labeling photographs in an album so your children and grandchildren will know about family members they never met. You may also choose to keep items that might be worth something after you pass away, so your family can sell them and have the money. If you notice things without value and that no one will want after you're gone, it's best to donate or discard them now.

With so many unique approaches to cleaning and organizing, you're sure to find one that suits your style. Just knowing of these methods can also help you get into the ideal mindset to start on your own belongings. Regardless of what you think of these approaches, the next segment will give you the basic steps you need to start your decluttering journey.

The Journey Forward

Every minute you spend looking through clutter, wondering where you put this or that, being unable to focus because you're not organized costs you: time you could have spent with family or friends, time you could have been productive around the house, time you could have been making money. –Jean Chatzky

As someone who has followed the steps in this book with varying degrees of success, I understand that decluttering can seem like a daunting task. However, I've offered many options throughout these chapters, so you're sure to find a method that works for you. I've tried many over the years, eventually creating my own hybrid approach that best helps my family keep our belongings minimal and our home organized.

While I love helping people organize their homes in person, this book will help you assess your belongings and understand what you need to do as if I were working alongside you. As you sort through things, you'll be able to determine what they offer you, whether it's something useful, like kitchen gadgets, or something you love, like a pillow that your grandmother made. In many cases, you'll find things that fit both requirements, like a cozy sweater your best friend knit. That's when the practical tips in this book will come to your rescue and help you decide what you need to keep and what you can do without.

I know it's hard to start decluttering, and I don't take the process lightly. It's why I addressed how to handle sentimental items in Chapter 2 and suggested different ways of storing them. If you feel like you need to get rid of anything that isn't practical, those sections will greatly help you. You can keep things that mean a lot to you and your family, whether you display them or keep them in storage boxes. You can even take digital photos and write your thoughts and memories so you can always look back on the items without having them physically in your home.

However, I'm sure you'll find satisfaction in sorting through your belongings and finding things you can donate or sell. I love when I find something I don't need anymore yet know one of my friends would love it. Seeing them wear sweaters or jewelry I didn't use makes me happy, and I appreciate what I kept even more.

There's no compulsion to only give your belongings to people you know. You can donate to a charity that aligns with your beliefs. They will give or sell your items to people who need and want them. You might also choose to sell some things yourself if they have value. Technology has simplified the process, so if you don't want to have a garage sale, you can sell things online. There are dedicated sale sites like eBay or Facebook Marketplace that make it easier than ever to ensure your unnecessary belongings find a new home.

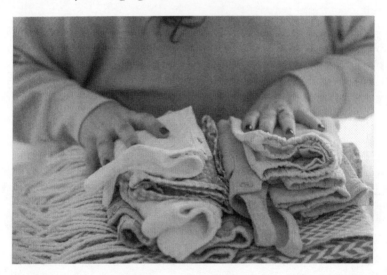

Once you declutter, you'll have information to help you organize and store your belongings to ensure they're out of the way and don't interfere with your minimalist home. As you appreciate the new look of your surroundings, you'll naturally pick up the minimalist mindset. Yes, the outward appearance of things is part of it, but you'll also find that you start needing fewer materialistic items. You'll focus more on the people you love and the experiences that make your life enjoyable. Instead of going shopping with your friends for fun, you'll enjoy having them over and talking for hours. Through this process, you'll start living intentionally and valuing experiences over possessions.

With the foundational knowledge and actionable tips in this book, I hope you'll be able to declutter your home and turn it into a place of peace and relaxation. Any time you feel like you need to refresh your surroundings, come back to the book and consider a different organizational approach or relook at my suggestions for sorting and organization. Whenever you feel stuck, this book will help you find a starting point that empowers you to take control of your surroundings and create the life you love.

And remember, habits in motion are habits in action, so the more you declutter, the more natural it will seem to keep up the good work!

Acknowledgments

To the love of my life, Iqbal Mutabanna, your unwavering support and gentle nudges ushered me onto this path. Without you, these pages would remain blank, and for that, I am eternally grateful.

To my parents, whose guiding light and unconditional love illuminate my path. I hope I make you proud.

To my heartbeats, my loving children, you inspire me every day. Being your mama is an honor, and it's the love for you that fuels my motivation.

To my dear sister, Zainab, whose diligent attention in shaping this book from inception has helped me stay the course. Thank you!

To my besties, Bhanu and Sunita. Your insights and suggestions were instrumental in shaping the outline of this book. Your wisdom and friendships are treasures I hold dear.

And to many of you who remain behind the scenes, the silent catalysts who breathed life into this project. Your support is immeasurable.

To all of you, I extend my heartfelt thanks. This book is as much yours as it is mine.

To all future readers of this book, thanks for giving my book a read.

References

Aguirre, S. (2023, June 29). *Here's how to conquer clutter with the 4-container method*. The Spruce. https://www.thespruce.com/conquering-clutter-the-4-container-method-1900130

Carson, K. (2019, January 8). *The "one minute rule" - decluttering your life*. KevinCarson.com. https://kevincarson.com/2019/01/08/the-one-minute-rule-decluttering-your-life/

Chun, K. T. (2020, December 2). Using the "one-minute rule" for a more organized and productive life. *Verily*. https://verilymag.com/2020/12/home-lifestyle-cleaning-organization-tricks-hacks

The danshari method; one of popular decluttering techniques in Japan. (2021, September 23). Japanmcconnell.com. https://japanmcconnell.com/the-danshari-method-one-of-popular-decluttering-techniques-in-japan-21034/

DiGiulio, S. (2017, November 2). *"Swedish death cleaning" is the newest decluttering trend*. NBC News. https://www.nbcnews.com/better/health/what-swedish-death-cleaning-should-you-be-doing-it-ncna816511

Dweck, C. S. (2006). *Mindset: The new psychology of success*. Random House.

Fallon, A. J. (2023, July 5). *How to use the "5S method" to organize your home*. Apartment Therapy. https://www.apartmenttherapy.com/how-to-use-5s-method-for-organizing-home-37271250

Fuller, K. (2022, June 30). *How clutter affects our mental health*. Verywell Mind. https://www.verywellmind.com/decluttering-our-house-to-cleanse-our-minds-5101511

Garrity, A. (2019, January 11). *What is the KonMari method? Here's how to declutter the Marie Kondo way.* Good Housekeeping; Good Housekeeping. https://www.goodhousekeeping.com/home/organizing/a25846191/what-is-the-konmari-method/

Grasmayer, B. (2018, February 21). *The 1 minute rule.* Wander Notes. https://medium.com/wander-notes/the-1-minute-rule-%EF%B8%8F-46c1c41050d5

Griffin, M. (2015, March 24). *How to declutter your life in 60 seconds: The one minute rule.* Melyssa Griffin. https://www.melyssagriffin.com/declutter-your-life/

Hage, J. (2019, October 8). *30 inspirational decluttering quotes you need in your life.* Filling the Jars. https://www.fillingthejars.com/declutter-quotes/

Hernandez, A. (2017, December 4). *The paper-free gift wrapping technique you need to try this year.* Apartment Therapy. https://www.apartmenttherapy.com/japanese-furoshiki-wrapping-technique-ideas-253297

Hopkins, E. (2023, January 7). *How to use the six-month rule when decluttering.* House Digest. https://www.housedigest.com/1160046/how-to-use-the-six-month-rule-when-decluttering/

Hudson, L. (2022, November 29). *I committed to this "kind" decluttering rule and it's helped me finally let stuff go.* Livingetc.com. https://www.livingetc.com/advice/six-month-decluttering-rule

カミラ [Camilla]. (2018, July 30). *Danshari - decluttering for A happier life.* Oishya. https://oishya.com/journal/danshari-decluttering-happier-life/

Kaplan, J. (2019). *How to use the KonMari method.* The Spruce. https://www.thespruce.com/the-konmari-method-4138610

Knierim, A. (2023, July 5). *Swedish death cleaning checklist*. The Spruce. https://www.thespruce.com/swedish-death-cleaning-4801461

Kondo, M. (n.d.). *About the Konmari method*. Konmari.com. https://konmari.com/about-the-konmari-method/

Lauster, N., McKay, A., Kwok, N., Yip, J., & Woody, S. R. (2016). How much of too much? What inspections data say about residential clutter as a housing problem. *Housing Studies, 31*(5), 519–539. https://doi.org/10.1080/02673037.2015.1094567

McGuirk, K. (2023, June 9). *6 Swedish death cleaning strategies to free you from clutter*. Better Homes & Gardens. https://www.bhg.com/decorating/storage/organization-basics/swedish-death-cleaning-tips/

Momber, A. (2022, October 13). *Here's how often you need to clean everything in your house*. Apartment Therapy. https://www.apartmenttherapy.com/house-cleaning-schedule-weekly-monthly-seasonal-annual-257612

Orr, D. M. R., Preston-Shoot, M., & Braye, S. (2017). Meaning in hoarding: Perspectives of people who hoard on clutter, culture and agency. *Anthropology & Medicine, 26*(3), 263–279. https://doi.org/10.1080/13648470.2017.1391171

Rogers, C. J., & Hart, D. R. (2021). Home and the extended-self: Exploring associations between clutter and wellbeing. *Journal of Environmental Psychology, 73*, 101553. https://doi.org/10.1016/j.jenvp.2021.101553

Santiago, D. (2020, March 23). *Four box method and self-storage: Making decluttering easy*. Easy Storage. https://www.easystorage.com/blog/four-box-method-and-self-storage-making-decluttering-easy

Sloan, D. (2015, July 2). *Is the "growth mindset" an agile mindset?* Scrum.org. https://www.scrum.org/resources/blog/growth-mindset-agile-mindset

13 methods for decluttering your home. (2021, January 18). Extra Space Storage. https://www.extraspace.com/blog/home-organization/home-organization-tips/methods-for-decluttering-your-home/

Thomann, L., & Nizam, A. (2020, March 3). *Too much stuff, not enough space? Try the 4-box technique.* Life Storage Blog. https://www.lifestorage.com/blog/organization/tackling-clutter-is-your-home-overflowing-with-too-much-stuff/

Thomas, M. (2023, May 10). *Why people can't stop talking about Swedish death cleaning.* Good Housekeeping. https://www.goodhousekeeping.com/home/organizing/a43826147/swedish-death-cleaning/

What is an agile mindset? (n.d.). www.wrike.com. https://www.wrike.com/agile-guide/faq/what-is-agile-mindset/

Whitney, J. (2022, November 20). *How the one minute rule changed my cleaning routine.* Simplified Motherhood. https://simplifiedmotherhood.com/one-minute-rule/

Image References

ATBO. (2016). *Closed gray and white wooden cabinet* [Image]. https://www.pexels.com/photo/closed-gray-and-white-wooden-cabinet-245204/

Chai, S. (2021). *Unrecognizable woman with folded clean baby clothes* [Image]. https://www.pexels.com/photo/unrecognizable-woman-with-folded-clean-baby-clothes-7282428/

Fotios, L. (2019). *White rolling armchair beside table* [Image]. https://www.pexels.com/photo/white-rolling-armchair-beside-table-1957478/

Grabowska, K. (2020). *Set of stylish cosmetic products placed near sink in bathroom* [Image]. https://www.pexels.com/photo/set-of-stylish-cosmetic-products-placed-near-sink-in-bathroom-4239017/

Lach, R. (2021a). *Hand picking up self care products organizer* [Image]. https://www.pexels.com/photo/hand-picking-up-self-care-products-organizer-10557498/

Lach, R. (2021b). *Hands of woman sorting clothes while sitting on floor* [Image]. https://www.pexels.com/photo/hands-of-woman-sorting-clothes-while-sitting-on-floor-10557481/

Lusina, A. (2020). *Person choosing document in folder* [Image]. https://www.pexels.com/photo/person-choosing-document-in-folder-4792285/

Milton, G. (2021). *Crop unrecognizable woman looking through printed photos* [Image]. https://www.pexels.com/photo/crop-unrecognizable-woman-looking-through-printed-photos-7015070/

Mubeena, Zohra. (2023). *Decluttered bedroom* [Image]. Provided by author.

Mubeena, Zohra. (2023). *Whiteboard with three columns* [Image]. Provided by author.

Mubeena, Zohra. (2023). *Whiteboard with two columns* [Image]. Provided by author.

Mutabanna, Azu. (2023). *Decluttered kitchen* [Image]. Provided by author.

Mutabanna, Azu. (2023). *Decluttered kitchen with plant* [Image]. Provided by author.

Pixabay. (2016). *Stack of towels on rack* [Image]. https://www.pexels.com/photo/baskets-clean-color-cotton-271711/

Rahubovskiy, M. (2021). *Living room with cozy chairs near lamp and wooden bookcase* [Image]. https://www.pexels.com/photo/living-room-with-cozy-chairs-near-lamp-and-wooden-bookcase-7195289/

RDNE Stock project. (2021). Boxes used for segregating things at home [Image]. In *https://www.pexels.com/photo/boxes-used-for-segregating-things-at-home-8581413/*.

Shuraeva, A. (2020). *Present wrapped with yellow fabric held by a person* [Image]. https://www.pexels.com/photo/present-wrapped-with-yellow-fabric-held-by-a-person-6305925/

Subiyanto, K. (2020). *Unpacked boxes in middle of room* [Image]. https://www.pexels.com/photo/unpacked-boxes-in-middle-of-room-4246091/

Summer, L. (2020). *Home interior with garments on racks* [Image]. https://www.pexels.com/photo/home-interior-with-garments-on-racks-6347888/

Made in the USA
Monee, IL
28 December 2023